A Time for

PLAYING

A **HOW ANIMALS LIVE** Book

A Time for

PLAYING

Ron Hirschi

PHOTOGRAPHS BY *Thomas D. Mangelsen*

COBBLEHILL BOOKS / Dutton
New York

For Anna Christine
—R. H.

For Karla
—T.M.

Library of Congress Cataloging-in-Publication Data
Hirschi, Ron.
    A time for playing / Ron Hirschi ; photographs by Thomas D.
Mangelsen.
    p.   cm. —(A How animals live book)
    ISBN 0-525-65159-4
    1. Play behavior in animals—Juvenile literature.   [1. Animals—
Play behavior.]   I. Mangelsen, Thomas D., ill.   II. Title.
III. Series.
QL763.5.H57   1994
591.51—dc20   93-36773   CIP   AC

Published in the United States by Cobblehill Books,
an affiliate of Dutton Children's Books, a division of
Penguin Books USA Inc., 375 Hudson Street, New York, New York 10014
Designed by Charlotte Staub
Printed in Hong Kong
First Edition 10 9 8 7 6 5 4 3 2 1

Chipmunk

Follow a chipmunk on its busy summer day.
Chipmunks nibble, chipmunks climb,
and chipmunks scurry.
Chipmunks are in such a constant hurry,
do they take time to play?

Chipmunk

Chipmunks run and chase, stopping to sniff,
nose to nose.

Play helps them know their neighbor.
Play helps them know who
is a friend.

Chipmunks

High up
in the branches,
tree squirrels play
on delicate limbs.
While playing, they learn
a path from tree to tree.
Play helps them
find a way to safety if
danger comes near.

Eastern fox squirrel

Ground squirrels play
down in their burrows
and out where the
wildflowers bloom.

When snow covers their
homeland, they might run
to catch up with a playmate
or run to find shelter
from the cold.

Arctic ground squirrel

Elk

Elk calves gather together
in meadows like soccer players waiting
for the game to begin.

But elk play is serious play—
they must strengthen wobbly legs
to outrun their predator,
the great grizzly bear.

Grizzlies search
with their eyes and sniff
the air too, hoping to find a meal
or a wilderness river where
bears can be bears.

Down in the river,
grizzlies can splash, run,
and dive.

Grizzly bear

Grizzly bear with cubs

Then up in the tall grass,
grizzlies stretch in the sun or
rub against one another to dry
after grizzly bear fun.

But no bears play
like polar bears play.

Polar bears

No bears dance like polar bears dance.

White as the blowing snow,
polar bears greet one another in the
frozen stillness and then their dance begins.
Polar bears roll, polar bears arch
long and strong necks.

Polar bears

Then they nuzzle and nibble
like puppies at play.
The polar bears dance together.
They also dance alone, a silent ballet dance
of the north in a faraway land.

Polar bears

Sea otter

Sea otters play when
they swim, diving for sea stars
or a bright-colored kelp crab.

They play with their food
to learn what is best.
But when they play with one another,
play can mean survival out on the cold ocean waves.

Otters comb and brush one another
in playful grooming up on the shore.
It must feel good to an otter to be fluffed,
to have shiny clean fur.
This fluffy coat traps air within the
otter's dense fur, insulating each otter from
bitter cold northern seas.

Sea otter

Sea otters

River otter

River otters
are sleeker, but
have lots of fat too.
They have no need
for combing and brushing
like their relatives
out at sea.

Always seeming to have
time on their hands,
otters play with one
another in water
and on land.

Otters stand up and chirp and tease others
to follow, or tumble and box like
kittens in your house.

River otters

Foxes play with one another or chase birds
they rarely can catch.
They try to catch magpie, a trickster
bird of the West.

Red fox

Kind of like a coyote, magpie tempts
and teases from a distance that is safe.
Then, fox tail fluffs and fox runs
as fast as foxes can run.

Do magpies know foxes can't fly?

Red fox chasing magpies

Lions

Play makes lions stronger,
zebras grow swift.

Burchell's zebras

Play helps baboons know one another.

Yellow baboons

But you don't have to take a distant safari to see animals play.

Hang a sunflower feeder up in your yard.
Birds will arrive,
but curious squirrels will too.

Eastern fox squirrel

Squirrels will jump and
squirrels will climb. And they
will playfully discover, one way or another,
how to get into what is not meant for them.

Just like you, squirrels learn as they play.
But maybe, just maybe, squirrels know
it just feels good to play.

Afterword

You probably never asked yourself why playing is so much fun. You just go outside or to your friends and play. People play at sports, we dance, and we play games that test our brains. Other animals may not play board games or spend a moment in front of a computer screen. But other animals play in many of the same ways and for most of the same reasons as people.

Play helps animals learn. Play strengthens young muscles. And play helps animals to become a part of the family and larger world. Animals will even play with members of a different species. Otters, for example, often tease ducks or coyotes. When they come in contact with our pets, they will also play with dogs.

Watch closely and you will see many animals playing in the air, on the waves, or in the trees. Like you, these playful animals probably don't ask why they play. They simply play.